"48 WHISPERS

From Pine Ridge and the Northern Plains"

THEBUSINESSOFSHAREDLEADERSHIP.COM

ISBN: 978-1-63758-062-2

Interior design and layout by Kourtney McLean | Published by Seventh Power Press in association with Post Hill Press

Post Hill Press
New York • Nashville
posthillpress.com
Published in the United States of America

Seventh Power Press
Casco, Maine
thebusinessofsharedleadership.com
Published in the United States of America

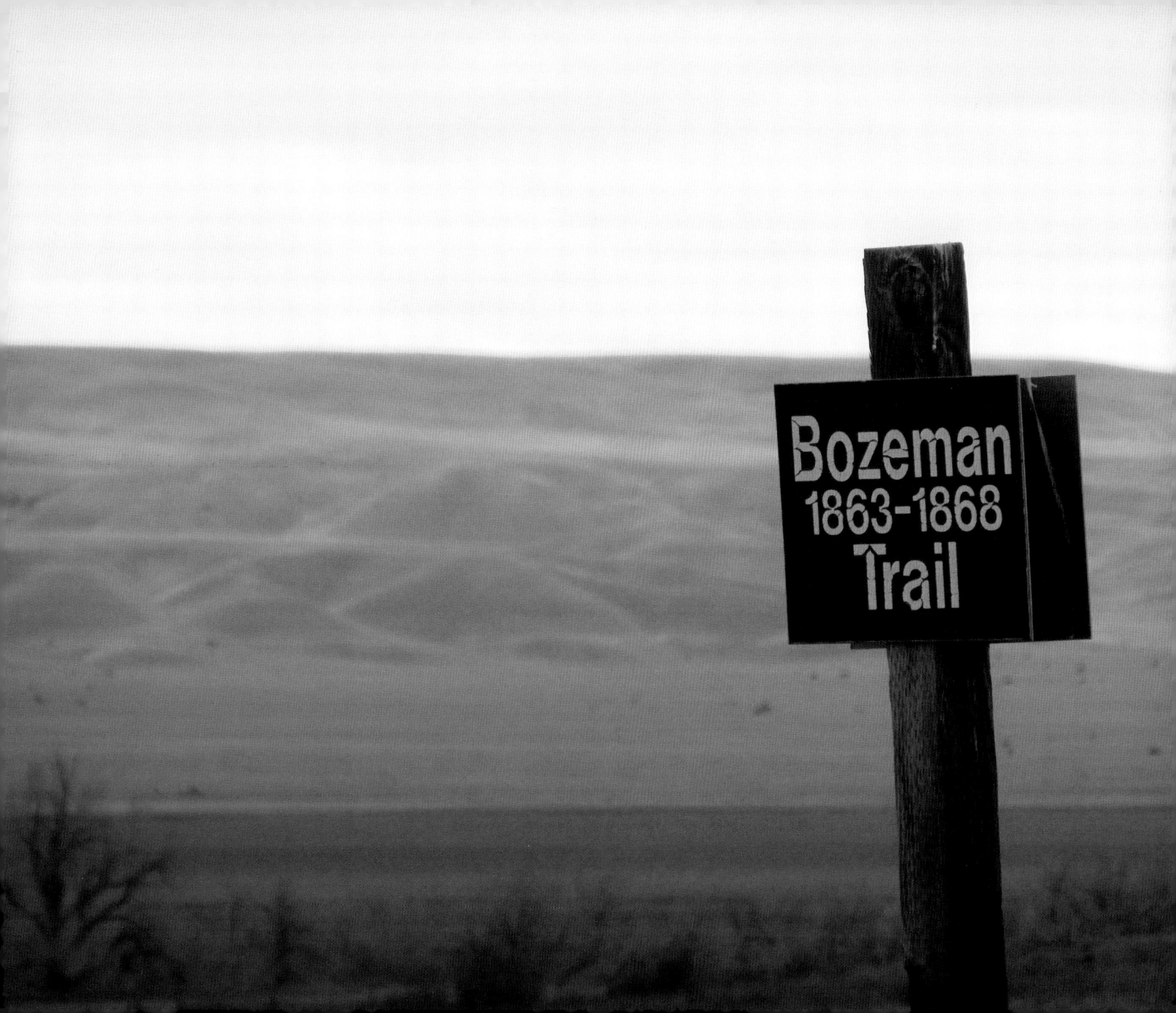
Bozeman
1863-1868
Trail

This book is dedicated to my daughters,
Abby and Sydney

and

to my Lakota big sister,
Catherine Grey Day

and

to the Singing Horse Trading Post

TABLE OF CONTENTS

Introduction....................8

Invitation....................26

This is the seventh generation....................30

Cross-cultural connectivity is reunifying....................32

What brings you here?....................34

"We are the truth we seek to know."....................36

We must become the change we seek....................38

In nature, power is dispersed....................40

Humans are a part of nature, not above it....................42

Mitakuye Oyasin....................44

Separateness is an illusion....................46

Division is a big business....................48

Everything travels in a circle....................50

You are the Seventh Power....................52

Leadership overreach has consequences....................54

Leadership restraint is about sharing power, not collecting it....................56

There are lots of ways to lose your voice in this world....................58

Listening is for understanding, not judgment....................60

We all adhere to a belief system....................62

Get out of your lane....................64

Selfish is self-less....................66

Great people are everywhere....................68

Culture makes the difference....................70

The Aquarian Age has dawned....................72

Localize and shrink the center....................74

For leadership to change, followership must change....................76

No zombies allowed....................78

It's time to rethink winning....................80

Half free isn't free....................82

Learn to embrace the art of healing....................84

Okay, now what?....................86

Love is the cure....................88

Isolationism doesn't work....................90

Watching the world through a screen distorts your view....................92

"When everyone shows up, it's time."....................94

Let's put work back in its place....................96

The dream is alive....................98

Endurance has a purpose....................100

Nature has acquired consciousness....................102

Awareness and connectivity are powerful acts....................104

Draw bigger circles....................106

Stay on your mission....................108

Conformity of thought kills alignment....................110

No one picks the date, time, and place of their birth....................112

Everyone picks the date, time, and place of their birth....................114

We are transitioning from physical to spiritual beings....................116

We are living in the age of the high-speed wobble....................118

We are the cause of the high-speed wobble....................120

The center is really everywhere....................122

What if everyone on Earth felt trusted, respected, valued, and heard?....................124

Excerpts from the Treaty of Fort Laramie (1868)....................128

Excerpts from Black Elk's Great Vision....................134

About the Author....................148

INTRODUCTION. I have lived my entire life in Maine, and while I come from a land full of trees, this book unfolds in a region defined by an endless sea of grass.

As a teenager our family took a vacation to the Grand Tetons. I was so enamored with the majestic grandeur of the West that I subsequently returned one college summer to work in Yellowstone National Park. I happily took a job as a housekeeper cleaning hotel rooms in exchange for the opportunity to hike the Yellowstone backcountry. During our days off we would hitchhike to trailheads and disappear into the wilderness. Whenever I came across a bison herd I was mesmerized. As a nineteen-year-old, I could sit and watch buffalo all day. I was in love with the American West.

But then I grew up and life began to call.

In 1998 I became president of Hancock Lumber, one of the oldest companies in America (1848).

In 2008 the national housing and mortgage markets collapsed, spiraling our industry and company into turmoil.

In 2010, at the peak of the economic crisis, I began to have trouble speaking. Suddenly all the muscles in my throat would spasm, squeeze, and contract when I talked. The simple act of verbal communication had unexpectedly become a complex chore. I was later diagnosed with spasmodic dysphonia (SD), a rare neurological voice disorder with no known cause or cure.

Trying to help lead our company through that crisis without the consistent or comfortable use of my voice took a toll, but at the time rest was not an option, so I fought through. I pushed and strained, despite my condition, all the way past 2012, when I could see that our company was going to be safe.

When it was over I intuitively recognized that I needed some time to focus on myself, regain my balance, and "search for my voice." How that restorative process unfolded, however, would exceed my wildest imagination. The West once again came calling.

––––––––––

In August of 2012 I picked up a copy of *National Geographic* magazine. On the cover there was a picture of a Lakota teenager riding a mustang across a treeless ridge. Below, the caption read:

In the Spirit of Crazy Horse
REBIRTH OF A SIOUX NATION.

Intrigued, I opened the magazine to page thirty and proceeded to devour the text:

"After 150 years of broken promises, the Oglala Lakota people of the Pine Ridge Reservation in South Dakota are nurturing their tribal customs, language, and beliefs. A rare, intimate portrait shows their resilience in the face of hardship."

Instantly I was fully immersed. I felt I knew this story somehow, and that I had been, or was destined to become, involved.

"I'm going to go there," I said to my wife, Alison, as soon as I had finished. "I want to see what life is like for the people who live there."

Three months later I was back in the American West, this time in the center of the northern plains. I disembarked from a small jet in Rapid City on a bright Sunday afternoon in late October, where Emma "Pinky" Clifford met me at baggage claim.

"Welcome," she said simply, as if she had been expecting me all her life.

Pinky was the executive director of the Oglala Sioux Tribe Partnership for Housing. I had contacted her during my initial search for a friend who might host my visit to Pine Ridge. After lunch we drove through the reservation for the first time. I was in awe of what I saw, simultaneously enthralled and confused.

That first trip triggered a host of deep emotions. I was captivated by the people of Pine Ridge. Their collective resilience despite historic tragedy and economic incapacitation was nothing short of inspiring. Additionally, I was transfixed by the northern plains. The enormity of nature was on full display here. The expansive grasslands, the rolling hills, the dusty outcroppings, and the proximity of sky to earth—all combined to sweep me away.

One trip became two. Two trips became three. In a span of eight years I would travel back to Pine Ridge and the surrounding plains more than twenty times. Here, usually alone, I could rest. Here I could breathe. Here I could turn inward. Here my voice improved. Here I felt as if I was truly present with all the world.

In the years that followed I would explore the entire reservation as well as the larger ancestral homelands of the Lakota people. From the North Platte River to the Yellowstone and from the Black Hills to the Bighorn Mountains, I would eventually cover nearly every road, abandoned fort, forgotten battleground, and historic trail in the region.

What I loved most was the experience of being nomadic.

I traveled light, carrying little more than a cell phone, a camera, a journal, and a wool sweater. Sometimes I knew where I was staying for the evening and sometimes I didn't. As the CEO of a corporation I was accustomed to schedules, routines, and deadlines, so this timeless and task-less odyssey felt liberating and otherworldly. At home I was well-known. Here, no one knew me. I traveled in complete freedom and anonymity. When something interested me, I stopped. When I was hungry, I ate. When tired, I slept.

Along the way I took picture after picture after picture, eventually collecting thousands of images. But what I did more than anything else was reflect. Ideas both cerebral and spiritual flooded my imagination. Here I could contemplate the past and the future with newfound clarity.

During my travels I became particularly interested in Black Elk, the most famous Lakota holy man of the twentieth century. In fact, I would visit the decaying cabin he once called home many times, and I even hiked one day to the summit of Black Elk Peak to perform a modest ceremony in his honor.

Black Elk's understanding—that sacredness dwells within us all—resonated deeply with me:

"The Wasichu wanted Crazy Horse to go to Washington with Red Cloud and Spotted Tail and others to see the Great Father [the president] there; but he would not go. He told them he did not need to go looking for his Great Father. He said: 'My father is with me, and there is no Great Father between me and the Great Spirit.' "

—Black Elk

The more I read about Black Elk, Lakota spirituality, and Lakota values, the more intrigued I became. There was a certain wisdom here that could only be obtained through generation upon generation of living and dying in intimacy with nature. This was knowledge from the soul of the universe personified and preserved by the Sioux, who then endured over a century of systematic oppression and genocide designed to erase then remake their presence on the plains. But through great hardship their knowledge, language, and culture endured.

As a visitor and a guest it was clear to me that the perseverance this required had a purpose. Their sacrifices were not in vain. The reservation communities of the northern plains had carried with them a wisdom from the past that was needed for the future.

This book aspires to honor that wisdom while paying respect to all the inhabitants of the northern plains, past and present, two-legged and four-. This book celebrates both the Indians and the ranchers, the nomads and the settlers, the residents and the passersby. For the storied history of this region is a microcosm of the entire human experience. Everything that exists is related and interconnected. There is a magical symmetry within the chaos of the universe, and this book walks that path.

Black Elk was escorted on his sacred vision by the 48 horses of the four directions. In honor of his journey, this book contains 48 thoughts (or whispers) for the future of humanity, each of which is 248 words in length. I use the term *whispers* because that is how each idea was received. It was as if the windswept grass spoke softly and shared a secret each time I stopped, sat still, and listened. As it turns out, these whispers are everywhere, but we are often too busy or consumed to hear them.

This is the third and final book in a trilogy that celebrates a decade-long odyssey that changed my life. That change was sparked by the people of the Pine Ridge Indian Reservation and then cultivated and refined by the magical aura of nature's hand on the northern plains. From here I'm moving on, deeper into the unknown, like nature always does, and as the people of Pine Ridge must now do.

Mitakuye oyasin. Please enjoy.

—Kevin Hancock

"I am drawn to the wild not because it is wild but because it is sensible, logical, ordered, stable, resilient. Wild nature is everything we're struggling to regain."

—Carl Safina

"Nothing can live well except in a manner suited to the way the power of the world lives and moves to do its work."

—Black Elk

*"Our ancestors knew that healing comes in cycles and circles.
One generation carries the pain so that the next can live and heal."*

—Gemma Benton

"You are an aperture through which the universe is looking at and exploring itself."

—Alan Watts

INVITATION. There are lots of ways to interact with a book, and in each case the reader's approach reigns. So engage this one as you see fit.

That being said, as the photographer, writer, and creator I would like to suggest a methodology that might otherwise go uncontemplated:

Slow down. Take a full YEAR to read, view, and absorb this book.

- First, turn all the pages in one sitting as you might with any photography book. Read a few passages, but focus mostly on the pictures and the flow. Consider this a perusal.

- When you're done, set this book in a quiet but visible place in your home where you retreat to relax. Let the book and its energy settle into that space, which is uniquely yours.

- Then return to this book once each week or so to read, contemplate, and meditate upon a single whisper. You can do this in order, or just randomly open to a page.

- When finished, write the title of that whisper on a piece of paper and put it in your pocket or set it on your desk. Put it somewhere where you will see it each day.

- Sometime during the week, should the willingness to share overtake you, visit my website (www.thebusinessofsharedleadership.com) and post your thoughts about that whisper. In this way each whisper will form a circle from me to you and back again. As other readers do the same, a dialogue may ensue; thinking may be furthered and refined. A ripple of change may be born and sent out into the world, to expand and develop.

Deep change requires contemplation and reflection before action can be sustained. My decade of travels to Pine Ridge stands as testimony to this truth.

Use this book, your Seventh Power, and the gift of time to create change—first, within you; then, beside you; and finally, beyond you. Surrender to the pace of this journey.

48 WHISPERS

From Pine Ridge and the Northern Plains

THEBUSINESSOFSHAREDLEADERSHIP.COM

Written and Photographed by Kevin Hancock

"This is the seventh generation."

WHISPER #1. Crazy Horse was born in 1842 near the Black Hills. In the decades that marked his life steamboats would conquer the Missouri River to the north as the railroad cut through the Platte River Valley to the south. All the while the buffalo herds kept shrinking.

For his people, Crazy Horse epitomizes the essence of Lakota resistance to white encroachment, and he is considered by many to be the greatest Sioux warrior of the nineteenth century.

Despite the cultural conflict, Crazy Horse prophesied reunification shortly before his death in 1877 (which he stated would unfold seven generations into the future):

"Upon suffering beyond suffering, the Red Nation shall rise again and it shall be a blessing for a sick world. A world filled with broken promises, selfishness, and separation. A world longing for light again. I see a time of seven generations when all the colors of mankind will gather under the sacred Tree of Life and the whole Earth will become one circle again. In that day there will be those among the Lakota who will carry knowledge and understanding of unity among all living things, and the young white ones will come to those of my people and ask for this wisdom. I salute the light within your eyes where the whole universe dwells. For when you are at that center within you and I am in that place within me, we shall be as one."

—Crazy Horse

Now is the time of the seventh generation.

"Cross-cultural connectivity is reunifying."

THEBUSINESSOFSHAREDLEADERSHIP.COM

WHISPER #2. I remember pacing the quiet halls of Chicago's O'Hare International Airport on an early Sunday morning as I waited for my connecting flight to Rapid City. It was my first trip to Pine Ridge and I was nervous. With no clear mission, I was setting out alone for the heart of Indian Country.

This was a leap of faith, and it felt like a bit of a risk. I was a lumber company CEO from Maine and there were no natural connections beyond a shared sense of humanity that linked me to the Oglala Sioux Tribe (OST).

Emma "Pinky" Clifford met me at baggage claim. She too was taking a risk. Pinky was the executive director of the OST Partnership for Housing. I had sent numerous e-mail inquiries to people and organizations at Pine Ridge, looking for a first friend who might host my visit, and Pinky was the only one to respond.

Her gesture of kindness and cross-cultural confidence paved the way for me to enter and access her community. I have now been there over twenty times, made dozens of friends, taken two Lakota names, and learned a lot about myself through a culture that is different from my own. All of that was made possible by Pinky.

I will forevermore be an advocate of cross-cultural connectivity. Connectivity is required both to honor our differences and to spark awareness of our similarities.

The challenges of race and racism cannot be transcended by any one single tribe.

"What brings you here?"

THEBUSINESSOFSHAREDLEADERSHIP.COM

WHISPER #3. It was the day before Halloween, and I found myself standing alone at the Wounded Knee Massacre site on the Pine Ridge Indian Reservation in the southwest corner of South Dakota. The sky was gray, the air was cool, and the highway behind me was empty as I paused before the red wooden sign that memorialized the events of December 29, 1890. On that morning four hundred and seventy soldiers of the Seventh Cavalry opened fire on Chief Big Foot's band of Miniconjou Sioux who had surrendered the night before without incident. The Lakota fought bravely but the killing was indiscriminate. There were few survivors.

As I contemplated the implications of this tragic encounter, a dusty sedan from a bygone era pulled up beside me. The driver, an old jewelry maker, rolled down her window and warmly proceeded to ask the simple question that changed my life: *What brings you here?*

This question sparks self-inquiry, demands intentionality, and invites us all to take control of the path we walk. It's a question capable of adding meaning to any moment in our lives.

I will never forget that jewelry maker's query, and to this day I wear the beaded eagle pendant necklace she sold me.

As for her question—it turned out I was traveling alone to the northern plains in search of my own true voice. Ironically, I was searching for my voice while visiting a community that did not feel fully heard.

That's what brought me here.

"We are the truth we seek to know."

THEBUSINESSOFSHAREDLEADERSHIP.COM

WHISPER #4. These words by philosopher Joseph Campbell reveal his understanding of the world's mythologies and sacred stories as manifestations of the inward-turning journey we are all called to undertake. While the external world is consuming, the gateway to our truth resides within. Life's great quest is to know thyself, thereby bringing forth your own unique voice. As Campbell writes:

"Heaven and hell are within us, and all the gods are within us. This is the great realization of the Upanishads of India in the ninth century BC. All the gods, all the heavens, all the worlds, are within us. When we simply turn outward, we see all of these little problems here and there. But, if we look inward, we see that we are the source of them all."

The Lakota vision quest rite, or Hanbleceya, is but one of many indigenous traditions designed to guide self-inquiry and strengthen our understanding that we must have peace within before we can walk in peace through the world.

I had my own vision-quest experience one day in the backcountry of Wind Cave National Park. From that experience four understandings were revealed:

- *You have what you need—enjoy what you have.*

- *You have made your own trail. You are your own person. Be at peace.*

- *You don't have to care for everyone else all the time; it's okay to do things just for you.*

- *We all have our own journey to make; let those around you make theirs.*

Inward lies the truth.

"We must become the change we seek."

THEBUSINESSOFSHAREDLEADERSHIP.COM

WHISPER #5. One of my dearest friends from Pine Ridge is Catherine Grey Day. She is a Dakota elder and a survivor of the genocidal boarding school era during which Indian children from across the plains were taken from their homes to be "remade" as whites. Native dress, language, and rituals were banned. Catherine, as a result, struggles to this day to fully speak her native tongue.

During my early visits Catherine was living in a trailer behind the Singing Horse Trading Post. It was here that two people who could easily have never met became friends, then family. Across numerous conversations Catherine would counsel me on my voice condition and the ways of the Great Spirit . . .

"Misunkala [little brother], it was you who opened your ears and heard Wakan Tanka speaking to you through others' voices, sending you to a beautiful place and beautiful people. Although we have suffered injustices, we find ways to live and survive. Wakan Tanka sends powerful spirit helpers. Keep listening to positive voices. We also learn from the negative. It is up to us to find balance. Our progress as a people must come from within."

Catherine's resilience, wisdom, and grace are inspiring to me. In return, Catherine has a new forum for her own voice to be heard. Despite all the external hardships she has endured, Catherine understands that true strength comes from within.

The first rule of change creation, it turns out, is knowing where to look for it.

WHISPER # 6. I was walking alone in the wilderness one evening when the epiphany I had been seeking materialized. It appeared suddenly, popping into my head in the form of five simple words:

In nature, power is dispersed.

Profound in its simplicity, this realization offered a long-awaited clue about the rightful place of shared leadership in human society. For a decade I had devoted myself to the development of a new management philosophy designed to strengthen the voices of others. "Everybody leads" had become my mantra.

This strategy had subsequently propelled our company to unprecedented heights while giving deeper meaning and purpose to the people who worked there. The appearance of this message instantly provided me with enhanced clarity, even certainty, that because this approach was aligned with one of nature's most sacred rules, it held favor over the long-standing tradition of top-down bureaucratic control.

In nature, power is dispersed.

"Of course," I whispered to myself with satisfaction. "That's it." Armed with this insight I began posing a series of questions to the natural scene that surrounded me.

"Where is the monolithic headquarters of this wild place? Where are all the managers and supervisors? Which of you scattered pines is in charge of all the others?"

My smile widened with each question as my confidence grew. I was on the right path. Nature was confirming it. The leadership power of nature is diffused by design. Humans, as a manifestation of nature's power, ultimately aspire to organize in this same way.

"Humans are a part of nature, not above it."

THEBUSINESSOFSHAREDLEADERSHIP.COM

WHISPER #7. Traditional Western thought often depicts humanity as nature's detached and isolated master. From this perspective the natural world surrounds but excludes us. It's a place we visit and tame.

The tribes of the northern plains have long held a different view.

Nowhere is this alternative vision better exemplified than with their traditional food source, the buffalo. Humans are the "two-legged" while the buffalo are our "four-legged brothers." This perspective infers a sense of relationship. For some of the four-legged to give their lives so that the two-legged might live is a sacred gesture.

"The buffalo knows you are coming for him," my friend Bamm Brewer told me inside his home near Slim Butte. I had recently completed my first buffalo hunt on the Wyoming plains near Pine Ridge. Two days later I brought the meat to the reservation and shared it.

The relationship between the Lakota and the buffalo is a reminder of an ancient indigenous understanding regarding our intimacy with the natural world. This awareness does not mean that we won't consume. In fact, to survive, we must. What it does mean is that when we consume, we must do so with reverence and a sense of connectivity, not greed.

Remembering that we are all manifestations of the same sacred energy source allows us to recognize that what we do unto nature, we also do unto ourselves. We are one of nature's countless iterations, and as such, we are irrevocably linked to the fate of the whole.

WHISPER #8. *Mitakuye Oyasin* is a Lakota phrase which translates to mean "All things are one thing" or "We are all brothers."

Everything that exists is not just connected—it's related. In fact, everything that exists is not just related; it's the same. The buffalo and its human hunters are comprised of the same sacred stardust. The recognition of oneness is present in most indigenous cultures. The Navajo call it *k'e*. I have a responsibility to all my relations, and I am related to all that I see.

Verola Spider, another cherished friend from Pine Ridge, is a third-generation storyteller. When I first began visiting the reservation, Verola worked weekends at the Singing Horse Trading Post while also teaching Lakota language at the Porcupine School and Oglala Lakota College. One Sunday afternoon as we sat together, she shared the following wisdom:

"Some of us, the old and real fluent speakers, we still believe that we are all related. When I am teaching in the classroom I try to teach that no matter what color a person is, we don't see the color. We see the spirit of the person and then we know that we are related. A lot of times you will hear people say, 'No, that's not the way,' but those people probably have a little bit of doubt in themselves. The truth is, we are all related."

It's transformational to recognize that everything we see is an extension of the same source.

Nature is a single being.

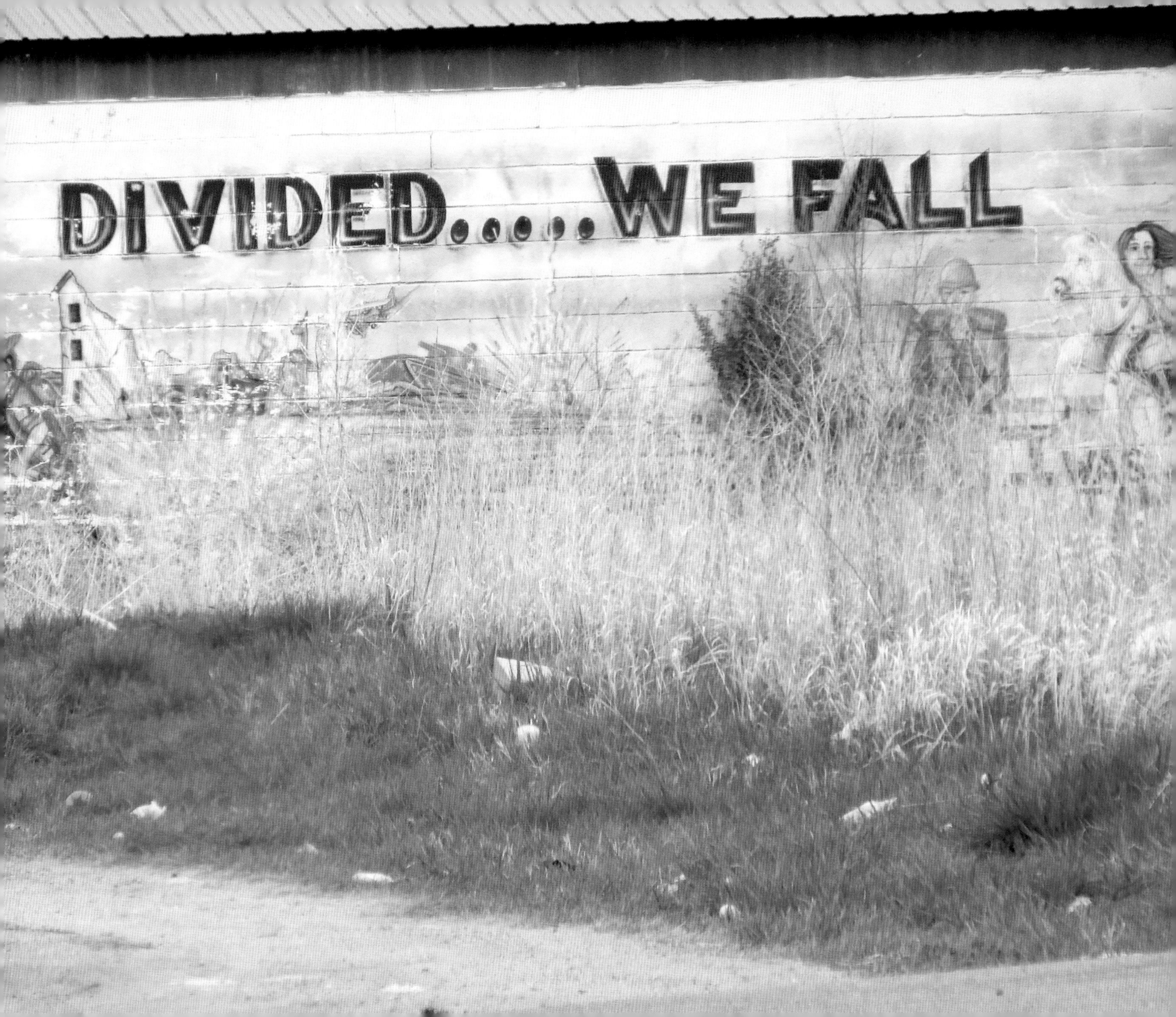
DIVIDED.....WE FALL

"Separateness is an illusion."

THEBUSINESSOFSHAREDLEADERSHIP.COM

WHISPER # 9. As I leave South Dakota and the Black Hills traveling west toward the Bighorn Mountains, I inevitably come upon a Welcome to Wyoming sign. The image depicts a cowboy, hat in hand, riding a bucking bronco in the shadow of the Grand Tetons. I stop each time and get out of my vehicle to contemplate this isolated border that invisibly divides a landscape oblivious to its existence.

Sometimes I imagine a Lakota caravan traveling west during a bygone era. They are headed for the hunting grounds along the tributaries of the Yellowstone River when suddenly they arrive at this curious sign. Puzzled, the nomadic community pauses as the elders discuss its meaning.

When the Oglala holy man Black Elk was born, this boundary line did not exist. When he died, it did. Which truth is real?

Each time I stop here there is not another person in sight. All I can see is golden grass, wooden fence posts, and barbed wire streaming toward infinity.

I contemplate a similar set of questions each time I leave Pine Ridge. Those reservation demarcation lines were originally created with nefarious intentions designed to isolate the Sioux until they could be remade as conforming Christian farmers. So what's the purpose of the reservation's borders today, and how long shall they last?

It is both important and liberating to recognize that many of the boundaries that surround us are only real so long as we imagine them to be so.

Separateness is an illusion.

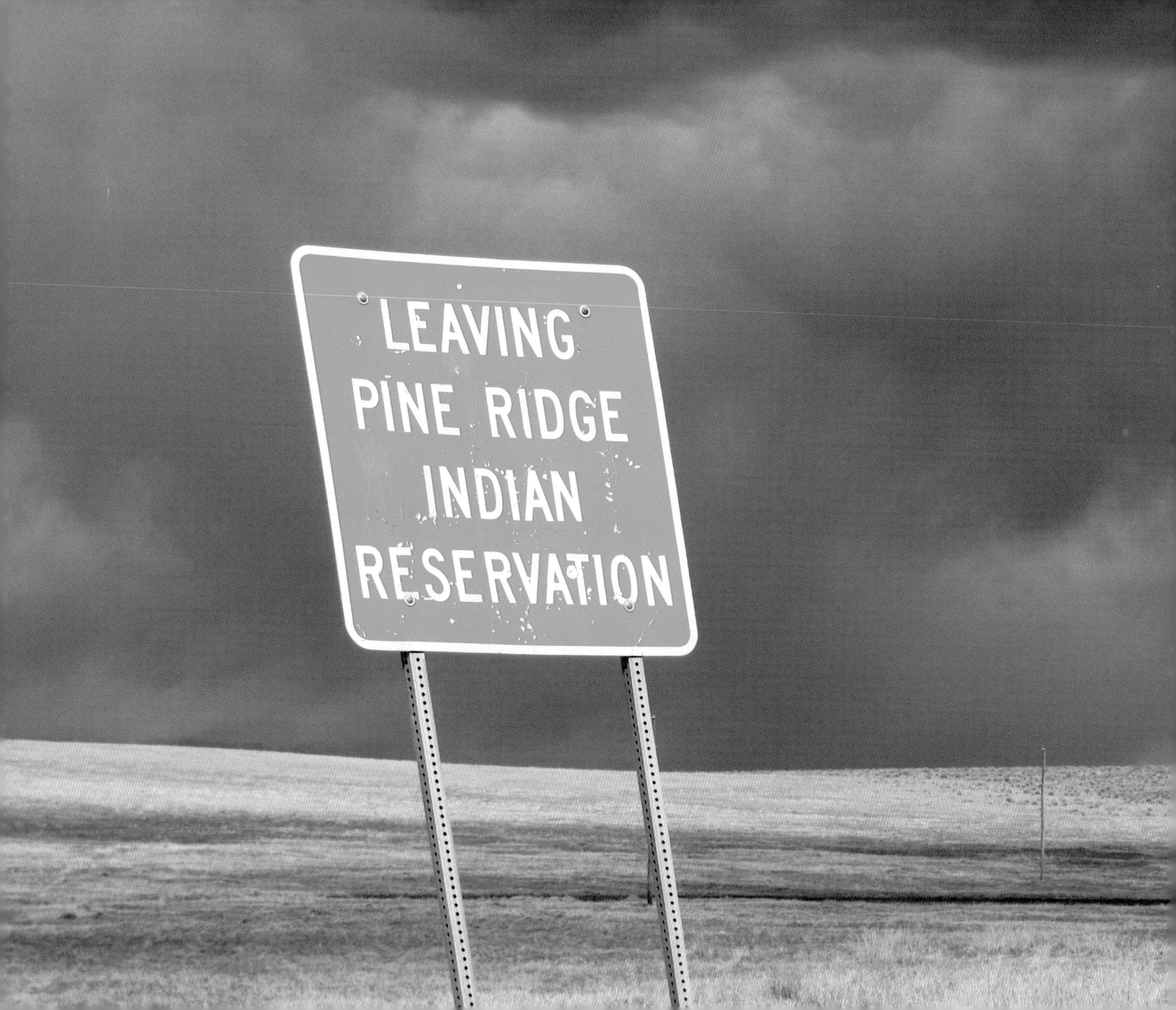
LEAVING
PINE RIDGE
INDIAN
RESERVATION

"Everything travels in a circle."

THEBUSINESSOFSHAREDLEADERSHIP.COM

WHISPER #11. One dichotomy on the northern plains is the quiet battle for supremacy between the circles and the squares.

The native tribes saw life as a never-ending sequence of circles, while the Euro-Americans constructed their world with straight and measurable lines.

One morning I walked the parade grounds of old Fort Fetterman in present-day Wyoming, which form a perfect square around the central flagpole. The remnants of this outpost serve as testimony to the orderliness of straight lines. Black Elk himself once referred to his reservation dwelling as "the square house they made me live in."

Black Elk further described his understanding of how the Great Spirit works in circles, not squares:

"Everything an Indian does is in a circle, and that is because the Power of the World always works in circles, and everything tries to be round. The sky is round, and I have heard the Earth is round like a ball, and so are all the stars. The wind, in its greatest power, whirls, birds make their nests in circles, for theirs is the same religion as ours. The sun comes forth and goes down again in a circle. Even the seasons form a great circle in their changing, and always coming back again to where they were. The life of a man is a circle from childhood to childhood, and so it is in everything where power moves."

When you learn to see the circles, you will better understand how power flows—including your own.

"You are the Seventh Power."

THEBUSINESSOFSHAREDLEADERSHIP.COM

WHISPER #12. The Lakota medicine wheel honors the six Great-Grandfathers through the six cardinal directions. Each direction represents a unique set of elements, factors, and forces that shape human life and the natural world. We are all impacted by that which surrounds us.

But the Lakota also recognize another great power that dwells within us all. It's called the "Seventh Power," and it represents the innate capacity of the individual human spirit. You are a magical force, for you also emanate from the creator. There are many powers shaping our world, and you are one of them.

This wisdom was shared with me just north of Sharps Corner at the headquarters of the Thunder Valley Community Development Corporation. Thunder Valley's mission is to attain economic and social independence through a return to core Lakota values and spiritual practices. I was visiting there one summer afternoon years ago when a friend held up a colorful medicine wheel and said the following:

"The axis running west to east represents the evil road of bad ways. The axis running north to south represents the good road to walk. The meeting place in the middle is called the 'Chokan.' The Chokan is the center of everything. It's the Seventh Power. The Chokan is you, standing in the middle of it all."

The Lakota medicine wheel honors the sacred power that dwells within us all. We are each a never-to-be-repeated manifestation of the Great Spirit.

You are the Seventh Power. Use it often, and wisely.

"Leadership overreach has consequences."

THEBUSINESSOFSHAREDLEADERSHIP.COM

WHISPER #13. Leaders often overextend themselves. Those with the most power frequently exercise it and go too far. This is overreaching, and it has consequences.

Each time I drive across the northern plains I am struck by the vastness of territory that is largely devoid of a human presence. There was, as it turned out, plenty of room for everyone here. Nonetheless, for decades upon decades Indians fought Indians, whites fought Indians, and whites fought whites for primacy and control of this land.

Leadership overreach is not limited to any single race, creed, or religion. It's a human temptation often exercised, always destructive, and never sustainable. Success for some has often come at the expense of others. The Lakota themselves were once conquerors. Subjugating weaker tribes and even taking slaves was all part of their expansion story, to—and beyond—the Black Hills. Likewise, overreaching was part of the American story. In the rush to claim our manifest destiny we denigrated and destroyed indigenous communities across the continent. Whoever had the most power on the northern plains often abused it.

In 1828, US Senator William Marcy coined the phrase "to the victor belong the spoils" in reference to wealth, territory, and possessions gained through conquest. This militaristic view of winning emboldens those with the most power to take what they please. Today Pine Ridge is the poorest place in America. That's not victory. The consequences of acquiring through defeating others ultimately haunt those who do it.

Overreaching always has consequences.

"Leadership restraint is about sharing power, not collecting it."

THEBUSINESSOFSHAREDLEADERSHIP.COM

WHISPER #14. Restraint is the opposite of overreaching. It's about having the most power but not using it.

Restraint is the essential leadership skill of the modern age. It's about giving strength to those who feel they have less power, and it's the only sustainable path to a fully engaged and accountable society.

I learned about leadership restraint through my voice disorder. As a CEO I was accustomed to using my voice to direct others. Suddenly talking was difficult and I was forced to do less of it. To protect my voice I began asking other people what they thought we should do. The answers I received were amazing, better than my own. I soon came to see my own speaking limitations as an invitation to give others a stronger voice. With this new understanding, our company began to soar.

Restraint is about leaders quieting down so that others can do and say more.

"We say that each child is *Wakan Yeja*," Verola Spider once told me. "It means 'sacred one.' Every child is sacred no matter when or where they enter this world."

If each child is sacred, then each adult is sacred. If each adult is sacred, then adult organizations should be structured accordingly. The truth is diverse, and finding it requires all voices. The full potential of the human experience can only be achieved by empowering everyone.

Ultimately, restraint is the manifestation of a deep confidence in others. Enlightened leadership is about making everyone else more powerful.

"There are lots of ways to lose your voice in this world."

THEBUSINESSOFSHAREDLEADERSHIP.COM

WHISPER #15. I once had a dream in which an angel offered to take me back in time fifteen years and start again.

"No! No!" I said to the apparition. "If we go that far back in time, I might not get my voice disorder again." I was adamant. I was unwilling to risk not acquiring spasmodic dysphonia (SD).

SD is a rare neurological disorder that only affects one's speech. In the years that followed onset the condition left me frequently unable to fully express myself verbally. I've since recovered substantially, but the healing journey spanned a decade.

Ultimately my voice condition brought me more benefits than liabilities. I came to see it as a welcome gift. It was an invitation for me to change and give others a voice.

I came to realize that there are many ways for people to lose a piece of their voice. As it turns out, lots of people don't feel authentically and fully heard. Without SD I never would have become sensitized to this reality.

Helping others to strengthen their voice is now a passion of mine, whether it is the simple act of listening at Pine Ridge or creating a work culture back home where leadership is shared. Developing the cultural conditions through which others might feel more fully heard is an act that requires everyone's participation.

There's a never-to-be-repeated voice that dwells within us all. Bringing it forth is every soul's quest. Supporting this fundamental right is also every soul's responsibility.

WHISPER #16. As a young manager I often listened to evaluate the perspectives of others. But after living for a few years with my voice condition the purpose of listening changed for me. Listening, it turned out, was for understanding. Authentic alignment only comes from honoring the diversity of views that exist naturally within the world. Voices are unique by design.

"Whose voice was first sounded on this land? It was the voice of the red people who had but bows and arrows. What has been done in my country I did not want, did not ask for it; white people going through my country. When the white man comes in my country he leaves a trail of blood behind him. I have two mountains in that country—the Black Hills and the Bighorn Mountains. I want the Great Father to make no roads through them. I have told these things three times; now I have come here to tell them the fourth time."

—Red Cloud

Conflict requires judgment. When judgment is the outcome of listening, no further progress is possible. When people are judged they don't feel heard and dialogue is rendered meaningless. When dialogue becomes meaningless, then force is often applied.

The nineteenth-century collision of America's Western expansion and the Lakota hegemony on the northern plains might have yielded a much different set of outcomes if everyone involved had been able to listen for understanding rather than judgment.

The only mind I need to open is my own.

" We all adhere to a belief system. "

THEBUSINESSOFSHAREDLEADERSHIP.COM

WHISPER #17. One morning in London, while doing research for my second book, I shared breakfast with a Colombian-born advertising executive, Jose Miguel Sokoloff. Over English tea Jose described the marketing campaign he had developed that enticed rebel forces in his native land to put down their arms and come home. In the process, he said something profound.

"We all adhere to a belief system;
otherwise, we don't have a strategy for dealing
with the world."

I soon found myself reflecting. What are the fundamentals of my own belief system, and how do they impact my view of the world? Is my personal narrative real, flawed, or both? Perhaps bringing change into the world is not about reorienting the views of others but rather refining my own lines of sight.

The Seeds of Peace Camp is located on a lake near my home in Maine. Each summer Arab and Jewish teenagers from the Middle East spend three weeks together at this rustic retreat. The program's pedagogy has produced a powerful saying: "We all have about half the story right."

Cross-examining one's own belief system can be unsettling. For America it would mean acknowledging that Columbus did not discover a new world; people already lived here. For the Lakota it would mean acknowledging their own expansionist past, where they too conquered others and built an empire.

Change is created by learning to question your own narrative, not someone else's. Recognizing you have a belief system is the key to transcending it.

"Get out of your lane."

THEBUSINESSOFSHAREDLEADERSHIP.COM

WHISPER #18. When I entered the world of business thirty years ago, "staying in your lane" was considered an expected practice for achieving corporate excellence. Success required maintaining a high level of focus on your company and industry. This insular philosophy was, and still is, commonplace.

Sustained attention to the details of one's craft is required for high-performing teams, yet staying solely in one's lane also creates disconnects, gaps, and lost potential.

Humanity needs more connectivity, not less. We need fewer silos and more corporations willing to expand their vision of purpose and responsibility. Advancing humanity should be every organization's goal, but that will require broadening our shared sense of mission.

We can no longer delegate or isolate ourselves from the planet's biggest challenges. Be it environmental health, a global pandemic, or racial bias, lasting solutions have a common theme: Everyone's participation is required. No enterprise should be too self-absorbed to engage in engineering social progress. The whole world is everyone's concern.

Across the past decade I have made more than twenty trips to the Pine Ridge Reservation and the northern plains. During that time, my professional performance improved and our company thrived. Many of my most valued ideas to help our company have come from getting away from it. Additionally, working beyond the boundaries of my industry has allowed me to broaden both my personal and corporate missions.

Staying in one's lane is the problem, not the solution. Switching lanes strengthens human connectivity, which, in turn, expands human capacity.

"Selfish is self-less."

THEBUSINESSOFSHAREDLEADERSHIP.COM

WHISPER #19. I once attended a powwow in honor of Tamokoce Te'Hila at the Prairie Wind Casino.

Billy Mills, as he is also known, is the most accomplished modern athlete to hail from the Oglala Sioux Tribe. His gold-medal run in the 10,000-meter at the 1964 Tokyo Olympics is still considered one of the greatest upsets in track history.

What I learned that night while listening to Billy speak was that he almost didn't try out for the Olympic team. The 1960s were a challenging time for reservation communities, and this was particularly true at Pine Ridge. Billy felt that leaving his home to race was perhaps a selfish act. In search of wisdom and advice he shared his conflicting emotions with several tribal elders.

"When you strengthen yourself, you honor your tribe," the elders told him. Billy was encouraged to run and run he did, bringing a gold medal home to the people of Pine Ridge.

The Seventh Power that lives within us all is meant to shine. Following your voice, talents, and inspirations is ultimately a selfless act. When you light up, the world around you becomes brighter. So follow your dreams and make yourself a priority. That which excites and captivates you is your gift to the world.

In Lakota spirituality the direction one faces is considered important. Each of us must strive to walk (or run, like Billy Mills) toward our own true light. Serving yourself honors your tribe, provides inspiration for others, and advances humanity.

"Great people are everywhere."

THEBUSINESSOFSHAREDLEADERSHIP.COM

WHISPER #20. In my early days at Hancock Lumber we had sweatshirts with our logo on them that read "Our People Make the Difference." Over the years I have seen this phrase connected with other organizations, as well. While I appreciate the spirit of the slogan, I have come to believe that it's not quite true.

Great people are actually everywhere. The planet, it turns out, is filled with them.

Everyone on Earth is a never-to-be-repeated gift to humanity, filled with the capacity for good. The tagline *Our People Make the Difference* implies that some communities are less successful because they don't have the "best" people. The very premise that certain groupings of people are better than others is filled with peril.

Better in what way?

Take the community of Pine Ridge, for example. For generations, before the arrival of the Wasichu (white people), the Oglala and other Lakota bands thrived. As a people (the *oyate*) they were self-reliant. Together they adroitly controlled a vast expanse of territory filled with wildlife and other resources. Today under the conqueror's imposed reservation system their community is the poorest place in America. Social challenges plague Pine Ridge, impacting young and old alike. Yet it's the same tribe in both settings. The Lakota have always been amazing, then and now.

The modern-day inhabitants of Pine Ridge are smart, caring, spirited, and resourceful, just like you. Great people are everywhere, including reservations. Therefore, it must be something else that makes the difference . . .

"Culture makes the difference."

THEBUSINESSOFSHAREDLEADERSHIP.COM

WHISPER #21. There is no one single nation or tribe that has cornered the market on great people. Great people are abundant and equally dispersed throughout the world.

So, what *does* make the difference? Why do some communities thrive while others struggle to survive?

The answer is culture. The culture of a community either disperses power or collects it into the bureaucratic center where the few hold sway over the many. Even a cursory look at history reinforces this pattern.

In the final days of World War II, American and British troops raced west across Germany as Russian troops pushed east. All understood that a divide would be created where the Allies met and that the fate of millions would hinge upon the resting point of an arbitrary line. West Germany, democratic and free, would go on to become one of the strongest economic engines in the world, while East Germany would fall into the autocratic orbit of the USSR, holding itself together with barbed wire and machine guns until it collapsed under its own monolithic weight.

So what was the fundamental difference between the two Germanys? Well, it wasn't that all the "best" Germans randomly ended up on the west side of the line. The entire country, both East and West, was filled with amazing humans. It was the governing culture that made the difference. West Germany would champion the individual human spirit while East Germany would conspire to thwart it.

Culture makes the difference. Great people are everywhere.

" The Aquarian Age has dawned. "

THEBUSINESSOFSHAREDLEADERSHIP.COM

WHISPER # 22.

"The world did not become round only at the point when it was acceptable to say it was round."

—Jan Fox

In 1633 Galileo Galilei was ordered to stand trial by the Catholic Church for believing that the Earth revolved around the sun. The Church maintained that humans sat at the center of the universe. To argue otherwise was heresy. Galileo was convicted, forbidden to teach, and relegated to house arrest.

Centuries earlier Pythagoras first hypothesized that the Earth was round, but it would take nearly one thousand years for this wisdom to become commonly accepted.

Both stories exemplify a defining characteristic of the Piscean Age (0 BC–AD 2000). The "truth" has often been carefully scripted and centrally defined.

But today we are living on the cusp of a new era. The Piscean epoch featured a centralized model of leadership in which people were governed through a web of deception and dogma. Conversely, the Aquarian Age now upon us is about the primacy of self and the innate capacity of the human spirit to determine one's truth and one's course. The symbol of this age is the water bearer—the water, a metaphor for knowledge that is being poured out and dispersed for all to use.

The Internet is a manifestation of this new template for shared power. So, too, is localized energy production, such as solar and wind power. In the Aquarian Age every individual is destined to become their own source of truth and light.

WHISPER #23. For centuries empires grew by amassing power into the center. "All roads lead to Rome," as the ancient saying goes. Dogma, coercion, force, and ritual overtly and covertly combined to keep large groups in rhythmic lockstep. But time is a stubborn thing. Strategies that sustained empires in one era can become their downfall in the next.

In the age of early man, localization ruled. Small bands united together for hunting, protection, and communal bonds. It was agriculture on a mass scale that allowed this to change. Suddenly large populations could assemble and become sedentary. No longer was everyone needed to secure food. From this new reality bureaucratic leadership emerged.

But in the twenty-first century, decision-making is aspiring to localize once again, and this dynamic favors a return to shared leadership. Autonomy of voice, agility of movement, and the sacredness of self are all ascending values.

Vibrant institutions of the future will increasingly flip the script on the centralized command systems of the past, and this will inspire entrepreneurial capabilities. Headquarters will learn to make themselves smaller and share the stage. Historically individuals have existed to serve the empire. Looking ahead, institutions will exist to serve their members.

As Rudyard Kipling wrote, "The strength of the pack is the wolf."

"For leadership to change, followership must change."

THEBUSINESSOFSHAREDLEADERSHIP.COM

WHISPER #24. If the new path to organizational excellence rests upon dispersed power, then followership as we know it must reinvent itself.

A follower is a person who moves or travels behind someone or something. But when the leaders learn to get out of the way, a fresh path will be cleared and illuminated for all.

The traditional philosophy of nation building required lots of followers, and entire societies were initiated into that orbit. The reservation system is one of many examples. The Lakota were required to report to their agencies and stay there during the last decades of the nineteenth century. Government agents and missionaries awaited, ready to teach tribal members to embrace a Euro-Christian agricultural path. Followership was the essence of this system. Someone else in a position of higher power had already determined what you should become. Free choice and the accountability that comes with it were not required attributes.

The rules of followership have long been etched into human societies. Children were seated in alphabetical order in classrooms that emphasized memorization and recital. At work, supervisors gave orders and employees did as they were told. Followership became a hallmark of good citizenship. This hierarchical dance has long been institutionalized and must now be carefully deconstructed.

As modern leaders learn to disseminate power, those accustomed to following must learn new skills. This will take courage. Reinventing followership requires us to trust in our own abilities, speak our truth, and embrace our shared responsibility for creating the future.

"No zombies allowed."

THEBUSINESSOFSHAREDLEADERSHIP.COM

WHISPER #25. I have been at Pine Ridge many times in late October. Halloween gatherings are organized in most communities across the reservation. Zombie-themed events are common and well attended, which always causes me to pause and reflect.

Why are zombie movies and television series so popular? I find these types of shows exceptionally predictable. No matter how many zombies you kill today, the horde returns for you tomorrow. The zombies themselves are dressed alike, cloaked in gray and indistinguishable.

Why the fascination?

Perhaps, deep down, we are all a bit afraid of becoming one.

A fictional Haitian and Creole creation, zombies unite en masse to form a mindless, monolithic, and inexhaustible army of destruction. The zombie is numb to independent thinking and incapable of feeling either joy or pain. Instinctively each zombie follows the group regardless of the destination or cause. Thirsty for blood, they attack without remembering why.

The Internet, social media, 24/7 news coverage, political divides, consumption-driven marketing, and the momentum of group thinking have the collective capacity to create a hypnotic buzz that numbs the senses and turns dialogue into a zombie trance–like monologue. We find ourselves talking without thinking or listening.

Awake, alert, and autonomous are the requirements that a sustained free society demands of us all. It's easy to follow, find, and target an enemy across the way and heap our problems upon them. But keep in mind that zombies rarely change their own condition by sacking and pillaging the lives of others.

"It's time to rethink winning."

THEBUSINESSOFSHAREDLEADERSHIP.COM

WHISPER #26. Having competed in sports and business my whole life, I understand the traditional view of winning. Winning is about supremacy and thus requires defeat. For every winner there must be an equal and corresponding loser.

The Roman Colosseum is an early manifestation of the consequences of losing. Here men fought to the death. For you to live someone else had to die. We can trace this primal reflex back to Joseph Campbell's summation: "Life eats life." Life endures by consuming itself.

Transcending ancient survival instincts is essential to advancing consciousness. In a world where we are all connected and related, winning is only winning if everyone advances.

My focus has been to bring a more holistic and sustainable view of winning into the world of work, commerce, and capitalism.

A company cannot win if employees lose. Conversely, employees cannot win if the company loses. Employers and employees either win or lose together. For a company to succeed, a "competitor" does not have to fail. That's finite thinking. Infinite thinking recognizes that the volume of success in the world can expand exponentially. There is no limit to the amount of happiness, love, and self-respect that humans can generate, give, or receive.

Winning is now collective. It involves us all. Armed with this alternative view of triumph, you no longer have to root against anyone. Helping anyone advances everyone. No one has to lose for you to win.

In the twenty-first century, winning isn't really winning unless everyone is advancing.

MASSACRE OF WOUNDED KNEE

Dec. 29, 1890, Chief Big Foot, with his Minneconjou and Hunkpapa Sioux Band of 106 warriors, 250 women and children, were [?] ped on this Flat, surrounded by the U.S. 7th Cavalry (470 soldiers), commanded by Col. Forsythe.

The "Messiah Craze" possessed many Indians, who left the vicinity of the Agencies to "Ghost Dance" during the summer and [?] 890. "Unrest" on the Pine Ridge Reservation was partly due to the reduction of beef rations by Congress, and to the "Ghost Dan[?] Chiefs Sitting Bull, Hump, Big Foot, Kicking Bear, and Short Bull. The Sioux were told by Kicking Bear and Short Bull that by [?] "Ghost Shirts", the ghost dancing warriors would become immune to the whiteman's bullets and could openly defy the sol[?] white settlers, and bring back the old days of the big buffalo herds.

On Nov. 15, 1890, Indian Agent Royer (Lakota Wokokpa) at Pine Ridge called for troops, and by Dec. 1, 1890, several [?] U.S. Regulars were assembled in this area of Dakota Territory.

On Dec. 15, 1890, Chief Sitting Bull was killed by Lt. Bullhead of the Standing Rock Indian Police. Forty of Sitting [?] escaped from Grand River, and joined Chief Big Foot's band on Deep Creek, to camp and "Ghost Dance" on [?] fo k of the Cheyenne River. Chief Big Foot was under close scrutiny of Lt. Col. Sumner and his troops, and [?] 23, 1890, they were ordered to arrest Big Foot as a hostile. However, the Big Foot band had already silently sli[?] [?] from the Cheyenne county, into the Badlands, heading for Pine Ridge.

On Dec. 28, 1890, without a struggle, Chief Big Foot surrendered to the U.S. 7th Cavalry (Maj. Whitesides) at the site [?] y a sign five miles north of here. The Band was then escorted to Wounded Knee, camping that night under guard. Reenforcements of the U.S. 7th Cavalry (including one company of Indian Scouts) arrived at Wounded Knee from Pine [?] cy the morning of Dec. 29, 1890. Col. Forsythe took command of a force of 470 men. A battery of four Hotchkiss [?] placed on the hill 400 feet west of here, overlooking the Indian encampment. Big Foot's Band was encircled at (OV[?]

[?]eator — Irving R. Pond and Herbert H. Clifford

By — Stanley S. Walker Sup. Highway [?]

Half free isn't free.

THEBUSINESSOFSHAREDLEADERSHIP.COM

WHISPER #27. The highest aspiration for mankind should be freedom for all. But freedom is elusive, tricky to define, and surprisingly hard to accept in all forms.

The absence of subjugation. The power of self-determination. The state of being unrestricted. These are common descriptions of freedom's lofty demands. But the pursuit of personal sovereignty comes with a price. The opportunity to succeed requires the corresponding right to stumble and fall.

There can be no freedom to earn more without the possibility of setback and loss. There is no opportunity to be selected without the potential of being passed over. There is no chance to earn an A without the corresponding presence of an F. The possibility of coming up short is freedom's price of participation. When we seek to eliminate the fall we inadvertently prevent the rise. True freedom makes space for all outcomes.

Additionally, the historic challenge posed by freedom is that some have expanded it for themselves by withholding it from others. This long-standing shortcut is occasionally alluring but always unsustainable. Many a revolution has achieved freedom for some and then proceeded to deprive it from others. Freedom for one requires freedom for all.

Free to succeed. Free to fail. Free to stumble. Free to prevail.

Freedom is not finite. Another's gain does not limit your access to freedom. The expansion of freedom for one advances freedom for all. Humanity's highest destiny is for everyone to soar. True success is additive to others. Anyone's progress helps us all.

"Learn to embrace the art of healing."

THEBUSINESSOFSHAREDLEADERSHIP.COM

WHISPER #28. Pain and trauma have been inextricably linked to the human experience. Setbacks and losses are universal. Everyone will be wounded. As a result, healing—the act of reconciliation and recovery—is perhaps the most important skill that humans can acquire. Yet where are the venues through which this critical capacity to recover is taught, cultivated, and nurtured? How do we learn to identify and transcend the wounds that dwell within us all?

First, we must look inward where the negative energy of all past injuries and injustice resides. While wounds are often inflicted or initiated by another, rarely can that offending party provide the cure. Instinctively it makes sense to look for healing at the scene of the crime, but wounding and recovering are separate acts. We often fail to heal because we look in the wrong place to find and release the residue.

Healing demands a willingness to journey within and stare vulnerably into the darkest corners of our past experiences. What is the true nature of my discomfort? What are the seeds of its origin? Am I ready to heal or has my narrative become too attached to the wound itself?

I made the decision a while ago to see my voice disorder as a gift, not a curse. Initially, I pictured healing as the restoration of my former voice, but in time I came to realize that healing is actually the opposite. Healing for me is the acceptance of my voice exactly as it is.

"
Okay,
now what?
"

THEBUSINESSOFSHAREDLEADERSHIP.COM

WHISPER #29. Confronting our authentic feelings about a past injustice is an important early step toward healing, but for enduring change to manifest, our introspection must ultimately transform into action.

Along the healing continuum a single question waits for us all:

"Okay, now what?"

This is the moment where you decide if you will make a move toward recovery, and, if so, in what form that initiative will manifest.

It's easy to demand action by another. Systemic social challenges require broad participation, but effectiveness can never be guaranteed when we wait for others to initiate the change we seek. Outsourcing the responsibility for altering your world is ultimately disempowering, as we become spectators of the actions taken by another.

Alternatively, you can make the next move. Becoming the action is liberating, as transformation is unleashed through the steps you take to bring something different into the world. Here, action is assured.

"Okay, now what?" is a question I often reflect upon at Pine Ridge, a community rightfully filled with grievances. The injuries inflicted here are deep and sustained.

But, okay—now what? What are the steps toward recovery, self-reliance, and change? Becoming the change is the only way to ensure that change occurs. There is always something that you can do right now to advance your position. Each positive step you take, no matter how small, nudges the future into a new arc.

When I change, the world around me transforms in the direction of the energy I bring forth.

WHISPER #30. I have a valued friend by the name of Gabrielli LaChiara. She is a healer who recovered from a potentially terminal cancer and now helps others do the same. Among her teachings is a simple yet transformative progression of thought with the capacity to heal all the wounds of the world:

Love is the cure.
You are love.
Therefore you are the cure.

Love is hate's opposing force. It is unifying, empowering, life-giving, and contagious. Hate cannot occupy a space filled with love. Hate requires the absence of love. You cannot hate something that you love. Love is the cure.

But where does love come from? What is its place of origin? Where is the house within which it resides?

The answers to these questions are known to every person on Earth. Love comes from within and it comes from us all. Love can be created in an instant and channeled toward anyone. Its capacity is infinite, and no opposing power can prevent it from forming. You are love.

Love is a choice you make over and over again. If everyone chose love, our world would change today. Love is the cure.

So how does love first form? It starts with the love of self. But what of our blemishes, missteps, and flaws, you ask? It turns out they are the purpose of love. Love transcends perfection and thus love heals. It's true what Gabrielli says:

Love is the cure.
You are love.
Therefore you are the cure.

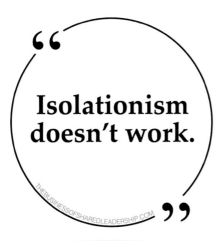

Isolationism doesn't work.

THEBUSINESSOFSHAREDLEADERSHIP.COM

WHISPER #31. In an uncertain world filled with chaos, diversity, and strife, isolationism has its advocates. If I retreat, perhaps I can be safe and secure.

But in an epoch defined by connectivity, isolation is a false haven. Isolationism doesn't work when there is no ability to isolate.

It takes fifteen hours for a human to travel from New York to Shanghai while a message can move between those cities in a matter of seconds. Two hundred thousand years ago all humans were relegated to a small geographic territory in Africa. In time our ancestors migrated and then eventually circled the globe, only to meet each other in the Americas in the fifteenth century with the belief they were separate tribes. Today transportation and information technology have combined to make us a single tribe once more.

There was a time when isolation worked. Space created safety. In fact, when Black Elk was a child, he "had never met a white man and did not know what one looked like."

Today, however, humanity's biggest challenges are trans-tribal and global in nature. Ours is a time when a virus can span the world in a matter of weeks. Isolationism is now an illusion.

Deeper engagement across cultures is what's required. Only by coming together can we combat threats and maximize opportunities. The poorest country impacts us all. The weakest health-care system is a shared vulnerability.

Castle walls once meant safety. Today they only increase risk by providing an illusionary sense of comfort.

"Watching the world through a screen distorts your view."

THEBUSINESSOFSHAREDLEADERSHIP.COM

WHISPER #32. If you read a news report summarizing the challenges at Pine Ridge you might well conclude that the situation is overwhelming. According to the well-regarded nonprofit Re-Member:

- The unemployment rate at Pine Ridge is 89 percent.
- The poverty rate is 54 percent.
- The high school dropout rate is over 70 percent.
- And 85 percent of families are affected by alcoholism.

If that dataset was all I knew about Pine Ridge, the challenges there would seem insurmountable. But I have been to Pine Ridge and I know the people who work at Re-Member. While the statistics are daunting, Pine Ridge in real life is a place filled with love, kindness, creativity, resilience, and inspiration. Make no mistake—there is sustained hardship and suffering, but there is also transcendence and triumph. Pine Ridge visited in person is a hopeful, energizing, and welcoming place.

Our 24/7 news coverage coupled with the seemingly infinite cacophony of social media can distort our view of the world. On most days, and in most places, life is more enjoyable and manageable than it appears on a screen.

As a child our television antenna connected my home to four stations. Each station broadcast thirty minutes of nightly national news. There was no Internet. Yet the adults of that generation were educated and engaged. Nonstop news does not enhance understanding; it distorts it.

The world in real life is a more hopeful place than it appears when condensed into sound bites and processed incessantly through a screen.

WHISPER #33. I once helped the Oglala Sioux Tribe build a home in a reservation community near the Nebraska border. Our company donated the building materials and then shipped them to Pine Ridge. I flew to meet the truck and to help unload it, knowing the freight company contractually allowed four hours to accomplish this task.

I arrived on-site at 8:00 a.m. ready to get to work, but no one showed up until 9:30 a.m., and it was after 10:00 a.m. before we started.

"Where is everyone?" I asked the first man on the scene.

"You're on Indian time," he told me with a smile. "When everyone shows up, it's time."

I'll never forget that moment, and its meaning has grown on me. In the business world that I am accustomed to, the clock rules the day. Everything is scheduled with a finite beginning and a certain end. I'm constantly checking my Outlook calendar to stay on task.

Pine Ridge moves at a different pace, one more connected to nature's flow. A visit begins when you arrive and ends when you leave. Schedules are rare. Moments seize themselves and there is a certain calmness that comes with this. I have never been hurried at Pine Ridge, and it's almost impossible to be late there. This provides the opportunity to be fully present, and that's part of what brings me back for more.

We pride ourselves on keeping track of time when learning to forget about it may be more valuable.

"Let's put work back in its place."

THEBUSINESSOFSHAREDLEADERSHIP.COM

WHISPER #34. Time is more than just an opportunity to be productive. This understanding is a gift I brought home with me from my excursions on the northern plains.

As a CEO I have tried to incorporate this wisdom into the world of work. As productivity improves, work should take less time, not more. Work should be important, engaging, and challenging—but it should not be all-consuming. As a work community we can use some of our productivity growth to make and sell more stuff, but we could also use a portion of that freed capacity to just plain work less.

Hancock Lumber has been able to reduce the average work week in our stores from forty-eight to forty-one hours while also increasing take-home pay faster than the national average. To do this we had to reinvent the traditional overtime pay system. Overtime pay is the worst possible financial incentive for the twenty-first century because it rewards just one outcome—making the work take longer. The real value-added goal is to find ways to make work take less time. A modern pay and bonus system should compensate for freeing time, not consuming it.

Reducing the employee's work week by seven hours creates more than eight weeks of suddenly freed time each year that every individual can reinvest as they see fit.

Putting the work back in its place can broaden human capacity. Productivity is a worthy goal when it triggers higher pay and more freedom for those who create it.

"The dream is alive."

TheBusinessOfSharedLeadership.com

WHISPER #35. I have read and heard that the American Dream is dead.

With this pronouncement comes the suggestion that it was easier to achieve success in past generations than it is today. I find this premise both doubtful and disappointing.

The notion of a uniquely "American" dream dates back to our nation's founding, and was often linked to the expanding frontier, including the northern plains. Was this dream really easier for pioneer families moving west by wagon and on foot, into an ungoverned land? Was it somehow easier for immigrant families arriving at Ellis Island in New York, carrying everything they owned in a suitcase? Was the dream easier for Native Americans growing up on reservations in the early decades of the twentieth century? Was the American Dream more achievable in the past than it is today? I doubt it.

The American Dream has always been about the possibility of tomorrow, a manifestation of the heart and mind. Additionally, that dream is more than just an economic exercise. To suggest that the dream can only be measured in inflation-adjusted dollars is to miss a giant swath of possibilities. What if I want to teach, or be a missionary, or write poetry, or become an organic farmer? It's neither fair nor accurate to say that only those who advance the most financially are living the dream.

The dream is about aligning your life with your own unique voice and aspirations. So dream on, America—the future is yours to create.

"Endurance has a purpose."

THEBUSINESSOFSHAREDLEADERSHIP.COM

WHISPER #36. I remember how I felt the first time I realized that genocide was part of the American story. It was another windy and searing summer afternoon, and I had just crossed the White River near the town of Interior, South Dakota. I pulled the car over and began walking in circles through the hardened dirt and grass. My shirt was off and my mind was reeling.

Moments earlier I had read the United Nations' definition of genocide.

"Genocide means any of the following acts committed with the intent to destroy, in whole or in part, a national, ethnical, racial, or religious group:

- *Killing members of the group.*

- *Deliberately inflicting conditions of life calculated to bring about its physical destruction.*

- *Forcibly transferring children of the group to another group."*

The hardships endured by the reservation tribes of the plains is a chilling story. But out of that collective tragedy some redemptive good for humanity has been preserved.

The Lakota are keepers of an indigenous wisdom that society desperately needs to incorporate. It's the kind of wisdom that comes from living in harmony with Mother Earth. We are of nature, not above it, and we must move, consume, and coexist in a manner that sustains and respects all life.

The plains tribes have endured generations of collective hardship and suffering. That journey had a purpose, and it was to provide an alternative view of our connectivity with Mother Earth, each other, and the Seventh Power, which resides inside us all.

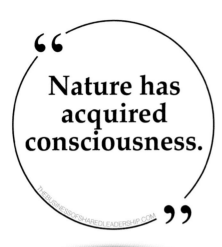

"Nature has acquired consciousness."

THEBUSINESSOFSHAREDLEADERSHIP.COM

WHISPER #37. During the COVID-19 pandemic I once heard someone rhetorically ask, *What if we are the virus?*

It was a hypothetical question. The speaker did not mean to suggest that it was literally true, but rather to offer a fresh perspective from which to view humanity's capabilities.

For a moment I could picture all the other creatures of Earth living in a time without humans. Then humans are introduced and everything changes. Humans are the alpha organism capable of dominating all of the other life forms. Like a virus, we spread and we spread. We cannot be contained. All that lives is dependent upon our restraint.

How we view ourselves has a lot to do with the choices we make. If nature exists to serve and supply mankind alone, that manifests into a certain set of outcomes.

But here's an alternative view: Humans are part of nature, not above it. Additionally, humans have acquired consciousness. Therefore, nature has acquired consciousness. Humans are nature's consciousness. If we are nature's consciousness, what responsibilities accompany that omnipotent role?

Not only do we have consciousness, we have also acquired one of the most sobering capabilities—the power to create and destroy.

What if we are nature, looking at itself? What if we collectively are the hand of God? What if, after billions of years of development, nature finally birthed an iteration of itself that could consciously act on its own behalf?

And what if this was the only thing we weren't conscious of?

Awareness and connectivity are powerful acts.

THEBUSINESSOFSHAREDLEADERSHIP.COM

WHISPER #38.

What do you do while you are at Pine Ridge?

This is a question I often receive back home in Maine. Initially I struggled to answer, but now I simply tell the truth.

"I don't really 'do' anything at Pine Ridge. I just spend time with the people who live there," I now reply.

Most nonnative people who visit Pine Ridge are government agents or nonprofit volunteers. There is typically a specific event or cause that brings them there. There's no agenda to my trips beyond being present. I travel to Pine Ridge because the place and its people give me strength. I meet people and listen to their stories. That's it.

Yet one day it occurred to me: Meeting people from another culture and listening to their stories is in and of itself an act of courage and change.

I see you. I appreciate you and I know what happened here. That's cross-cultural connectivity, and anyone can foster it. All it takes is the willingness to get out of our comfort zones.

Marginalized communities don't need to be fixed, saved, or changed by people from away. They simply need to be respected, heard, understood, and empowered. The people of Pine Ridge are amazing exactly as they are, and they hold all the power they need to create change for and within themselves.

I still see the difficulty and the pain. But even more clearly, I see the humanity and the light.

Awareness and connectivity are powerful acts.

"Draw bigger circles."

THEBUSINESSOFSHAREDLEADERSHIP.COM

WHISPER #39. It is delicate to not be Indian and yet write about Indian Country. *Only Indians should speak for Indians* is a common phrase I have heard at Pine Ridge and try to honor.

But to whom do the challenges at Pine Ridge belong? Is reservation life an Oglala, Lakota, Sioux, Indigenous, North American, or human concern? Who gets to care about and commit to advancing the future of this community?

From the vantage point of the moon, everything on Earth would look like a human problem. So I guess the answer depends on how one chooses to draw their circles. I prefer to see a single human tribe.

In all my years of writing about my experiences there, I have never attempted to speak for anyone but myself. In fact, this book is not about the northern plains but rather about how I have been influenced by the reservation and the surrounding region.

The people of Pine Ridge are important to me and the plains have been transformative for me. There I feel my connectivity to the oneness of the universe and the unifying potential of Mitakuye Oyasin. With each visit I bottle these feelings and bring them back home.

The first time my friend Catherine Grey Day and I met, she said, "When we look at someone, we don't see the skin color—we see the goodness of the heart. I can see you have a good heart."

Let's back our view up and draw bigger circles.

"Stay on your mission."

WHISPER #40. The current state of American political discourse has a negative impact on society's ability to engage in productive dialogue and respect the views of others. It's loud, denigrating, and non-collaborative—pretty much the exact opposite of what we would like our elected leaders to mentor and model.

So one day I just decided to stop listening. I turned them all off.

Why? Because I have my own mission that I want to advance, which is showing respect for all voices, and I'm not willing to be deterred from that pursuit by someone else's negative energy.

Our political system has several systemic problems: First, it's a zero-sum game. I must defeat the opposing party to be victorious. Second, the incentives are short-term. Humanity's challenges require long-term focus, yet our electoral system runs in two-year increments. Finally, the drama gets 24/7 coverage. The more outrageous the rancor, the more attention one receives.

What happens in Washington is important, but it shouldn't be all-consuming. Approximately 330 million people live in America, yet only 537 of them are elected to serve in the House, Senate, and White House. Ultimately, it's what the non-elected do that defines our country.

In the age of 24/7 news, Twitter, Instagram, and Facebook, the ability to stay focused on your own mission is foundational to personal health and effectiveness.

I claim my energy as my own. Aware, yes; distracted, no. Transcending diversions is my Buddha-like responsibility. In an age of constant noise, you still control the dial.

"Conformity of thought kills alignment."

THEBUSINESSOFSHAREDLEADERSHIP.COM

WHISPER #41. Imagine a scene from a totalitarian regime rally in a great square before an imposing granite capital. The entire gathering chants in unison and the collective will seems insurmountable. But we all know that's neither alignment nor consensus. That's leadership intimidation, overreaching, and excessive control. It's those with the most power restricting the voices of others.

Self-centered organizations have often pursued a single truth recited by all. But that's an unsustainable mission pursued by dogmatic and self-serving empires. Voices are meant to be unique by design. Excessive conformity restricts freedom. True synergy only manifests from the presence of a diversity of views and the acceptance of all voices.

In order for people to say what they truly think, the culture of their community must be safe. For dialogue to be safe we must refrain from judging what others say. It's only when people feel safe that they will let down their guard and open themselves to introspection and new ideas. The only voice any of us should shape is our own.

Diversity of thought is essential to a free and healthy society. It's the conformity of thought that kills alignment. It may feel tempting to eradicate thinking that's fundamentally different from our own, but in the end, either everyone is free to speak or no one is. A far better skill is to be able to state the views of others to their satisfaction without feeling threatened or compromised.

A great country tolerates a wide range of voices.

"No one picks the date, time, and place of their birth."

THEBUSINESSOFSHAREDLEADERSHIP.COM

WHISPER #42. No one should be judged by the date, time, and place of their birth.

The house we are born into is a dynamic that none of us can control, yet virtually everyone is labeled to some degree by their unique point of entry into this world. Thus, it is ironically easy to describe people that we don't actually know.

My experiences at Pine Ridge have been transformative in this regard. Across dozens of trips to the reservation I have come to know lots of people there. As a result, I see what systemic oppression does to a community filled with otherwise amazing human beings. In the absence of this direct connectivity I would likely make many incorrect assumptions about the people of the Rez.

Many residents of Pine Ridge are low-income, so that must mean they aren't hardworking.

The school dropout rates are high, so that must mean education is not valued there.

I know that these assumptions are not true because of the time I have invested in getting to know the people who live there. Their community, just like yours, is filled with thoughtfulness, resilience, love, and talent.

I hope my time at Pine Ridge has broken the barriers of assumption in two directions. As a statistic, I am the white male CEO / 1 percent guy that you read about. It would be equally easy to label me—unless we've met.

No one should be judged by the date, time, and place of their birth.

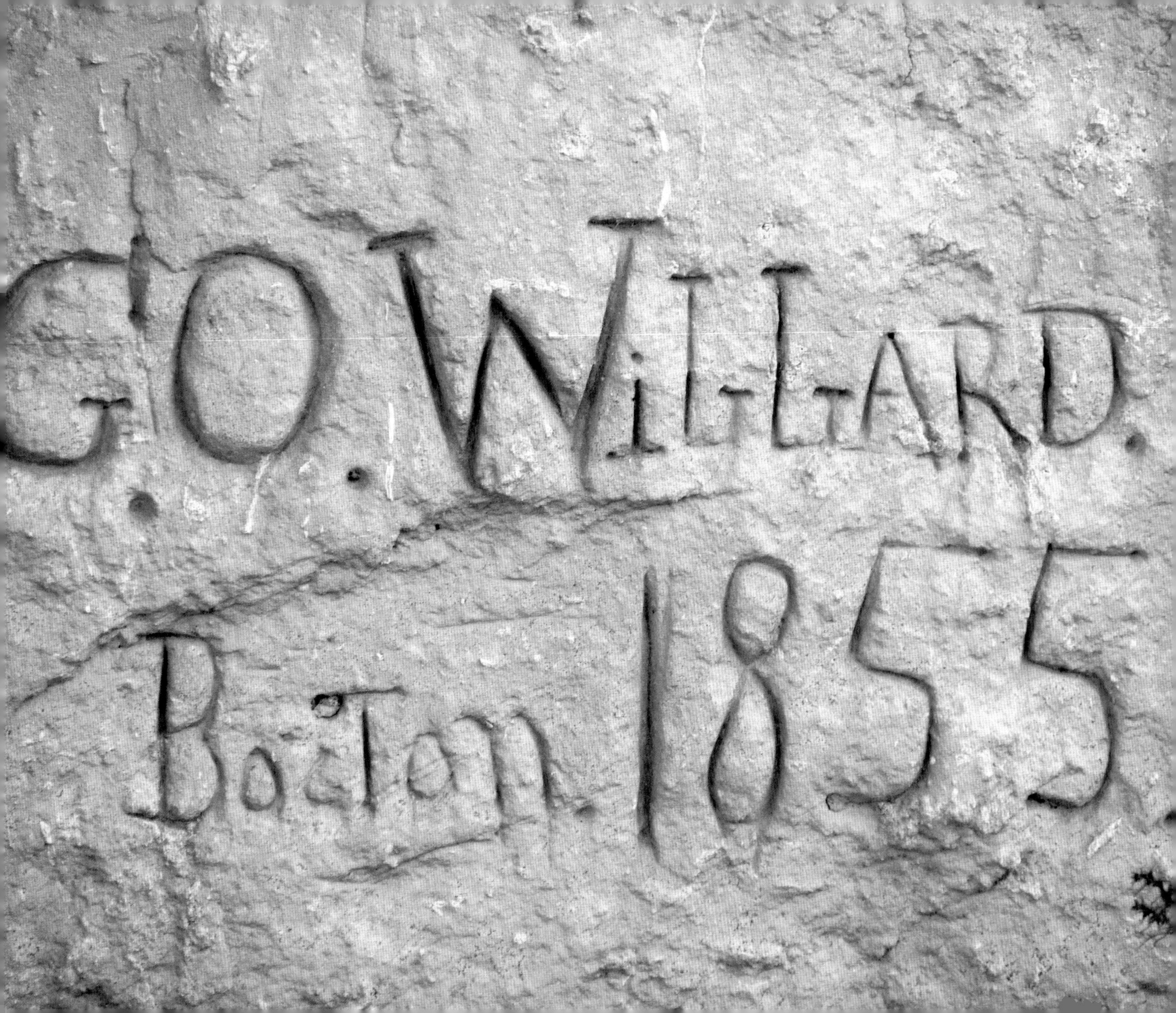
G.O. WILLARD
Boston 1855

"Everyone picks the date, time, and place of their birth."

THEBUSINESSOFSHAREDLEADERSHIP.COM

WHISPER #43. I have a friend and mentor by the name of Deborah Dooley. She is a clinical psychologist and evolutionary astrologist from the San Francisco area.

Evolutionary astrology has three tenets that run parallel in many ways to indigenous spirituality. The first is that everything that exists is related and interconnected. It's all comprised of the same stardust. Second, this stardust or sacred energy has a mission. It wants to evolve. It wants to learn, grow, and advance to a higher state of being. Third, when it comes to humans, the soul is the transcendent being (the body is more like a vessel). Human souls have multiple incarnations across time for the purpose of evolving.

What if we did select our point of reentry with intention? What if certain life experiences were designed to call forth the learning we seek to acquire in this lifetime?

That's a lot to digest, but just for a moment, pretend it's the case.

How might this hypothetical truth alter your view of your past and present condition? How might it impact your interactions with a spouse, sibling, coworker, or friend? What if everyone *did* pick the date, time, and place of their birth? How might that change the way we see and engage the world around us? What if life's experiences were karmic lessons we signed up for in disguise?

Would you see the world with fresh eyes if this were the case? Perhaps it's worth pretending that it's so . . .

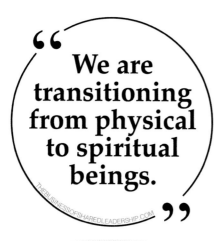

"We are transitioning from physical to spiritual beings."

THEBUSINESSOFSHAREDLEADERSHIP.COM

WHISPER #44. There is a metamorphosis playing out across human history that's hard to see because it's exceptionally slow.

We are transitioning from physical to spiritual beings.

Early human history was defined by short lives and the day-to-day struggle for survival. It was kill or be killed. Eat or starve. The world that surrounded prehistoric humans was dangerous and required constant survival energy. Weekends, hobbies, vacation, and retirement were all constructs that would not be realized for eons.

Despite how you might feel on certain days and despite the trauma all humans still endure, there is significant change occurring, and the transformation is accelerating before our eyes.

In 1900 the average human life expectancy was thirty-one. In 2017, it was seventy-two.

In 1776 the typical agricultural work week was close to eighty hours. In the 1840s the average American factory worker spent sixty-eight hours on the job. Today the average work week in the United States is forty-four hours.

Humans are living longer, working less, and acquiring time. With this transition comes the opportunity for reflection, service to self, and the capacity to transcend mere survival mode. As the physical dimension becomes easier to navigate, we shift toward the spiritual plane. We are evolving. We are a species in transition.

Human progress is not linear, and not all cultures, communities, and individuals are equally safe and secure. By expanding the conditions of safety for more people, we accelerate the spiritual journey for all.

We are spiritual beings in physical form.

"We are living in the age of the high-speed wobble."

THEBUSINESSOFSHAREDLEADERSHIP.COM

WHISPER #45. In 2001 nineteen militants associated with Al-Qaeda hijacked four airplanes and brought society to a sudden halt.

In 2008 the housing and mortgage markets collapsed, propelling the world into a perilous economic depression.

In late 2019 several visitors at a seafood market in Hunan Province, China, gave flight to a virus that would create a global pandemic.

That's three destabilizing events of epic proportion in just two decades. None of them were predicted or forecast. In each case the world changed in a matter of months, weeks, and even days.

Scattered between these exceptionally disruptive events have been periods of general economic strength and prosperity. Stability to instability and back again; that's the wobble of the twenty-first century.

What does this mean for human institutions like families, corporations, and nation-states? It means we all need to be ready to withstand a pause, navigate chaos, and adjust.

Under such circumstances, how does anyone build a personal or business financial model spanning a single decade? How does one plan for retirement? How do corporations forecast investments or plan for expansion? Debt and risk take on a new level of precariousness when the cliffs of destruction keep appearing without warning along an otherwise lovely country road.

We are all connected. There is nowhere to hide. Instability anywhere is instability everywhere. This is why we must slow down, move with thoughtfulness, and identify win-win strategies that benefit everyone. Either everyone's okay or no one's okay in the century of the high-speed wobble.

We are the cause of the high-speed wobble.

THEBUSINESSOFSHAREDLEADERSHIP.COM

WHISPER #46. When our company first began learning about lean manufacturing practices, we worked with a talented consultant named Lisa Westberg. As she reviewed each of our core operating systems she would ask, "Is it stable, or are we about to go into a high-speed wobble?"

Excessive speed, frantic motion, and the absence of early warning systems that are powerful enough to stop production are the ingredients that can tip a community (or an entire planet) into chaos.

Does all of this sound familiar?

It should, because it's what has happened to Planet Earth in the early decades of the twenty-first century. What are the foundational underpinnings of 9/11, the housing market collapse, and the COVID-19 pandemic? The answer: excessive speed and motion. Humans are moving at a pace that is unsustainable in what business researcher Jim Collins defines as "the never-ending pursuit of more."

How many people can we pack into an airplane? How short can we make the turnaround time at the gate? When speed and capacity take precedence over the quality of an experience, a wobble is sure to follow.

When the COVID-19 pandemic reached Maine, our company eliminated all nonessential activity. In hindsight, I was amazed at how many tasks and trips we were able to do without. When we slowed down, our business performance actually improved.

Humanity needs to pump the brakes, put quality of life first, and reset at a sustainable pace. Less movement increases stability.

We are the cause of the high-speed wobble.

"The center is really everywhere."

THEBUSINESSOFSHAREDLEADERSHIP.COM

WHISPER #47. For centuries scientists, spiritualists, and philosophers have attempted to discover the center of all that is. The sun revolves around the Earth. No, wait; the Earth revolves around the sun. And what of the universe itself? Where is its center?

So what does the concept of center even represent? In geometry the center is the middle of the object. In social terms, it is the place of gathering.

But what if the center is really everywhere? What if the center, like the power of nature itself, is scattered and diffused? If the center was everywhere, where would that place you? What if you are the center?

Black Elk foretold all of this long ago:

"The first peace, which is the most important, is that which comes within the souls of people when they realize their relationship, their oneness, with the universe and all its powers, and when they realize that at the center of the universe dwells Wakan-Tanka, and that this center is really everywhere, it is within each of us. This is the real peace, and the others are but reflections of this."

Black Elk came to understand that the center we so desperately seek lives within us. This realization is the path to sustained peace. The implications of this truth cannot be overstated.

The center, it turns out, can be found without taking a step. We need but look inward to find the peace we seek.

Sleep well, my friend. You are already at the center.

"What if everyone on Earth felt trusted, respected, valued, and heard?"

THEBUSINESSOFSHAREDLEADERSHIP.COM

WHISPER #48. Given all the work that goes into enhancing the human experience, why isn't humanity advancing faster? Perhaps it's because there is no unifying mission to our work. Ego and tribalism divide, and our planet is still dominated by both.

How many widgets can a company produce? How much territory can an empire acquire? How many converts can a religion muster? These questions all bring me back to the northern plains during the second half of the nineteenth century, when we nearly killed all the buffalo.

Why did we kill virtually all the buffalo? Money, greed, ego, tribalism, and capacity. What if every human organization (be it private, public, secular, or spiritual) adopted a shared mission? Just what might that mission be? I suggest the following:

Let's help every person on Earth feel trusted, respected, valued, and heard.

If everyone on Earth felt trusted, respected, valued, and heard, what might change? I think everything might change. The center is everywhere. It lives within us all. As a result, progress can only be achieved by helping individuals to find their center and thereby activate their Seventh Power.

Human organizations need a new mission—one that is bigger than their own industry, territory, ego, or god. As long as we are working for a subset of humanity, humanity will continue to be divided. A better goal could change all of this.

Help others feel trusted.
Help others feel respected.
Help others feel valued.
Help others feel heard.

This is the mission.

It's been an enlightening joy to create friendships and even familial bonds with people at Pine Ridge.

It's been equally rewarding to introduce friends and family from my own tribe to the Oglala Sioux and the northern plains.

—Kevin Hancock

Excerpt from the Treaty of Fort Laramie (1868)
Article 1

"From this day forward all war between the parties to this agreement shall forever cease."

ON THIS FIELD ON THE 21ST DAY OF
DECEMBER, 1866,
THREE COMMISSIONED OFFICERS AND
SEVENTY SIX PRIVATES
OF THE 18TH U.S. INFANTRY, AND OF THE
2ND U.S. CAVALRY, AND FOUR CIVILIANS,
UNDER THE COMMAND OF CAPTAIN BREVET-
LIEUTENANT COLONEL WILLIAM J. FETTERMAN
WERE KILLED BY AN OVERWHELMING
FORCE OF SIOUX, UNDER THE COMMAND OF
RED CLOUD.
THERE WERE NO SURVIVORS.

Excerpt from the Treaty of Fort Laramie (1868)
Article II

"The United States agrees that the following district of country commencing on the east bank of the Missouri river where the 46th parallel of north latitude crosses the same, thence along the low-water mark down said east bank to a point opposite where the northern line of the State of Nebraska strikes the river, thence west across said river, and along the northern line of Nebraska to the 104th degree of longitude west from Greenwich, thence north on said meridian to a point where the 46th parallels of north latitude intercepts the same, thence due east along said parallel to the place of beginning shall be set apart for the absolute and undisturbed use and occupation of the Indians herein named."

Excerpt from the Treaty of Fort Laramie (1868)
Article XII

"No treaty for the cession of any portion or part of the reservation herein described which may be held in common, shall be of any validity or force as against the said Indians unless executed and signed by at least three-fourths of all the adult male Indians occupying or interested in the same."

Excerpt from Black Elk's Great Vision

"Now and then the voices would come back when I was out alone,
like someone calling me,
but what they wanted me to do I did not know."

Excerpt from Black Elk's Great Vision

"I was lying in our tepee and my mother and father were sitting beside me. I could see out through the opening, and there two men were coming from the clouds headfirst like arrows slanting down. They came clear down to the ground and stood a little way off and looked at me and said:

'Hurry! Come! Your Grandfathers are calling you!' "

Excerpt from Black Elk's Great Vision

"And the oldest of the Grandfathers spoke with a kind voice and said: 'Come right in and do not fear.' And as he spoke, all the horses of the four quarters neighed to cheer me. So I went and stood before the six, and they looked older than men can ever be—old like hills, like stars."

Excerpt from Black Elk's Great Vision

"The oldest spoke again: 'Your grandfathers all over the world are having a council, and they have called you here to teach you.' "

Excerpt from Black Elk's Great Vision

"Now I knew the sixth Grandfather was about to speak, he who was the Spirit of the Earth, and I saw that he was very old. But more as men are old. His hair was long and white, his face was all in wrinkles and his eyes were deep and dim. I stared at him, for it seemed I knew him somehow; and as I stared, he slowly changed, for he was growing backwards into youth, and when he had become a boy, I knew that he was myself with all the years that would be mine at last. When he was old again, he said: 'My boy, have courage, for my power shall be yours, and you shall need it, for your nation on the Earth will have great troubles. Come.'"

Excerpt from Black Elk's Great Vision

"Then I was standing on the highest mountain of them all, and round about beneath me was the whole hoop of the world. And while I stood there I saw more than I can tell and I understood more than I saw: for I was seeing in a sacred manner the shapes of all things in the spirit, and the shape of all shapes as they must live together like one being. And I saw that the sacred hoop of my people was one of many hoops that made one circle, wide as daylight and as starlight, and in the center grew one mighty flowering tree to shelter all the children of one mother and one father. And I saw that it was holy."

Excerpt from Black Elk's Great Vision

"I could see my people's village far ahead, and I walked very fast, for I was homesick now. Then I saw my own tepee, and inside I saw my mother and my father bending over a sick boy that was myself. And as I entered the tepee, someone was saying: 'The boy is coming to; you had better give him some water.' Then I was sitting up; and I was sad because my mother and my father didn't seem to know I had been so far away."

(Excerpts taken from *Black Elk Speaks: Being the Life Story of a Holy Man of the Oglala Sioux* as told through John G. Neihardt.)

"The sacred energy of the Universe is dispersed. It lives within us all. Strengthening a sense of power in others is the true calling of a great leader. A tribe is made strong one individual at a time.

—KEVIN HANCOCK

THEBUSINESSOFSHAREDLEADERSHIP.COM

ABOUT THE AUTHOR. KEVIN HANCOCK is an award-winning author, speaker, and CEO, and an advocate of strengthening the voices of all individuals—within a company or a community—through listening, empowering, and shared leadership.

Kevin is a recipient of the Ed Muskie Access to Justice Award, as well as the Habitat for Humanity Spirit of Humanity Award.

Established in 1848, Hancock Lumber is a seven-time recipient of the Best Places to Work in Maine Award. The company is also a recipient of the Maine Family Business of the Year Award, the Governor's Award for Business Excellence, the MITC Exporter of the Year Award, and the Pro-Sales National Dealer of the Year Award. The company is led by its 550 employee associates.

Kevin's first book, *NOT FOR SALE: Finding Center in the Land of Crazy Horse*, won three national book awards. His second book, *THE SEVENTH POWER: One CEO's Journey into the Business of Shared Leadership*, was published in 2020 and is distributed by Simon & Schuster.

Kevin continues to be a frequent visitor to the Pine Ridge Indian Reservation in South Dakota.

Kevin is a graduate of Lake Region High School and Bowdoin College. He lives in Maine with his wife Alison.

For more information, or to contact Kevin, visit
WWW.THEBUSINESSOFSHAREDLEADERSHIP.COM

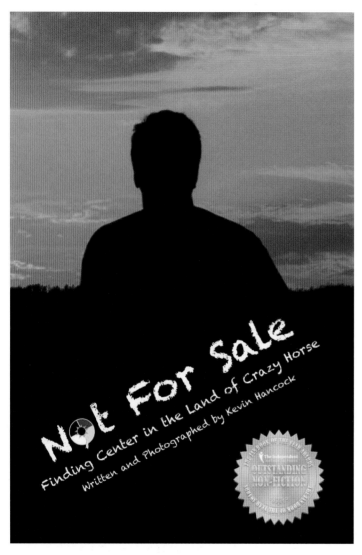

NOT FOR SALE: Finding Center in the Land of Crazy Horse is a unique icono-clastic memoir that traces one businessman's journey deep into Indian country, and even deeper into his own soul. In a corporate world hallmarked by the never-ending quest for bigger, better, more, this CEO of one of America's oldest companies learns to look inward for meaning and purpose.

What readers are saying about NOT FOR SALE . . .

"I finished reading your book a couple of days ago and found myself not wanting it to end. I'm a firm believer that there are no coincidences. Your book is one of those rare gifts that have been placed into my life."

"I'm not even sure how to put into words what I'm feeling while reading your book. The truth is, I'm only halfway through, but felt an urgency to write to you. Not only did I feel like I was sharing in your spiritual journey, but I also feel like my heart has been opened to an entirely different point of view and understanding. I found myself reading a page (and in some cases, a single sentence) and then having to stop and process the message I just read. I've been asked by others what book I am reading, and am finding it hard to express my internal feelings into voiced words when explaining not only what I'm reading, but how it is speaking to me."

"I read your book in two days because I simply couldn't stop. I kept putting it down, and within two or three minutes I was back at it. Your book is both mesmerizing and life-changing."

"I read Not For Sale: Finding Center in the Land of Crazy Horse *in record time. I simply couldn't put the book down. Your courage in sharing your vision quest is so beautiful—a true inspiration."*

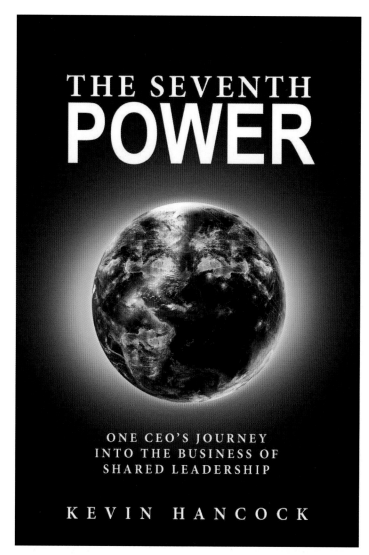

THE SEVENTH POWER: One CEO's Journey into the Business of Shared Leadership. A corporate executive loses his voice and discovers a new pathway to organizational excellence built on the premise of dispersed power and shared leadership. Kevin Hancock's personal journey holds universal messages for people at all levels of business and community. The Seventh Power's new, more-inclusive approach to leadership and management will give you important insights into your life, your career, and your company.

What readers are saying about THE SEVENTH POWER . . .

"What a book! Your message is wonderful and important, more vital than ever in these challenging times. Our world needs these leadership insights."

"I wanted to reach out and say thank you! I recently finished your book and absolutely love it! I have since read it again, this time with a pencil in hand. In all honesty, this will be the first book I have ever reread from front to back. There are so many parts throughout that resonated with me, and I couldn't help but feel the need to take a deeper dive!"

"I am writing to express my appreciation for your book. My only complaint is that you didn't write it sooner. For if I had implemented your Seventh Power beliefs earlier in my life, I would not have burned out mid-career with health issues and stress. Keep up the great work!"

"After your book, I know I personally need to work on giving more space to my team and to building a better environment for them to personally grow and thrive. Your belief that we can and must utilize business as a way to make a cultural change in the world has transformed my thinking about my company and my role as a leader. Thank you!"

"When we try to pick out anything by itself, we find it hitched to everything else in the universe."

—John Muir

"Transcending the urge to judge, fix, solve or transform others is what actually creates the conditions for communities or companies to progress. When people feel heard, not judged, they relax. When people relax, they think. When people think, they grow."

—KEVIN HANCOCK

"Across human history, power has been centralized. But, like anything that travels in a circle, it can be given back. The fundamental building block of personal power is self-worth—the internal knowing that you are sacred."

–Kevin Hancock